Building An
Intimate Relationship
with your
Heavenly Father

Building An Intimate Relationship with your Heavenly Father

Godwin Browne

XULON PRESS

Xulon Press
2301 Lucien Way #415
Maitland, FL 32751
407.339.4217
www.xulonpress.com

© 2022 by Godwin Browne

All rights reserved solely by the author. The author guarantees all contents are original and do not infringe upon the legal rights of any other person or work. No part of this book may be reproduced in any form without the permission of the author.

Due to the changing nature of the Internet, if there are any web addresses, links, or URLs included in this manuscript, these may have been altered and may no longer be accessible. The views and opinions shared in this book belong solely to the author and do not necessarily reflect those of the publisher. The publisher therefore disclaims responsibility for the views or opinions expressed within the work.

Unless otherwise indicated, Scripture quotations taken from the King James Version (KJV) – *public domain.*

Paperback ISBN-13: 978-1-6628-4708-0
Ebook ISBN-13: 978-1-6628-4852-0

Dedication

This book is dedicated to the Christians who are not serious about their relationship with their heavenly Father. My prayer is that this book will encourage you to become serious and start building an intimate relationship with your heavenly Father.

It is only when we have an intimate relationship with our heavenly Father that life really becomes more meaningful and fulfilling. We will begin to reflect what our heavenly Father is like in all we do and say. Our Father is looking for people who will represent Him on earth. When we become intimate with Him, then we will be able to represent Him well and show the world who He really is.

Introduction

One of the definitions for the word "intimate" is having a close friendship or relationship. That is what our heavenly Father wants us to have with Him. Our Heavenly Father is always concerned with relationships when it comes to His dealings with man. He had relationships on His mind when He made man and placed him in the Garden of Eden. He came down and had fellowship with the humans because He loved them and the relationship they enjoyed was important to Him. As we build an intimate relationship with our Heavenly Father, He will direct our paths in the right direction and bring success to our lives.

Contents

Chapter One: Benefits of Intimacy 1
Chapter Two: Abraham, a Friend of God 5
Chapter Three: How to Build an Intimate
    Relationship with God 17
Chapter Four: The Secret Place with God 27
Chapter Five: Knowing God in a Real Way 33
Chapter Six: An Intimate Walk with God
    Produces Fruit 41
Chapter Seven: The Intimacy of Jesus and His Father . . 51
Chapter Eight: Intimacy Between God and Moses 57
Chapter Nine: Living in the Presence of God 63
Chapter Ten: Be Flexible In the Hand of God 69
Chapter Eleven: The Holy Spirit and Intimacy 75
Chapter Twelve: The Increase of the Anointing 81

CHAPTER ONE

Benefits of Intimacy

When we make the decision to have an intimate relationship with our heavenly Father, there are many benefits to derive from it.

Job 22:21-28:

> *Acquaint now thyself with him, and be at peace: thereby good shall come unto thee,*
>
> *Receive, I pray thee, the law from his mouth, and lay up his words in thine heart*
>
> *If thou return to the Almighty, thou shalt be built up, thou shalt put away iniquity far from thy tabernacles.*
>
> *Then shalt thou lay up gold as dust, and the gold of Ophir as the stones of the brooks.*

Yea, the Almighty shall be thy defence, and thou shalt have plenty of silver.

For then shalt thou have thy delight in the Almighty, and thou shalt lift up thy face unto God.

Thou shalt make thy prayer unto him, and he shall hear thee, and thou shalt pay thy vows.

Thou shalt also decree a thing, and it shall be established unto thee: and the light shall shine upon thy ways.

Our journey of intimacy with God begins with getting acquainted with Him. To get acquainted with God is to get to know Him through His Word. As we spend time reading and meditating on the Word, it gets deep into our spirit, and our live becomes ordered by the Word. The Word brings light into the dark places of our lives and life to the dead areas of our lives. The Word will help us to see who God really is, and it will enable us to get closer to Him in our relationship.

When we are well-informed about our heavenly Father, the Devil cannot mislead us. Additionally, the peace of God will reign in our hearts. This is a peace that the world cannot take away. As we receive the Word from Him, it will give us confidence to be intimate with Him.

When we are intimate with Him, we listen to Him when He speaks, and we obey Him. If we stray away from Him, He will always make Himself available to restore our relationship with Him.

Intimacy causes our prayer life to be effective. God will answer us speedily and what we decree will be established in the realm of the spirit. Our Father's ears are always open to hear the cries of His children so He may answer their prayers and meet their needs. Intimacy gives us confidence in God. Confidence gives us boldness to speak the Word of God and makes the Devil afraid of us.

Psalm 16:5-11:

> *The Lord is the portion of mine inheritance and of my cup: thou maintenest my lot.*
>
> *The lines are fallen unto me in pleasant places; yea, I have a goodly heritage.*
>
> *I will bless the Lord, who hath given me counsel: my reins also instruct me in the night seasons.*
>
> *I have set the Lord always before me: because he is at my right hand, I shall not be moved,*

Therefore my heart is glad, and my glory rejoiceth: my flesh also shall rest in hope.

For thou will not leave my soul in hell; neither wilt thou suffer thine Holy One to see corruption.

Thou wilt show me the path of life: in thy presence is fullness of joy: at thy right hand there are pleasures for evermore.

To be intimate with our heavenly Father is a conscious decision we have to make. We have to be determined in our hearts that we will live a life of intimacy with our heavenly Father. When we do this, we can enjoy the rich blessings that He will shower on us. Intimacy with God makes God our portion and our inheritance. When He is our portion and our inheritance, this puts us in a wealthy place. This is what will happen when we are determined to be intimate with God.

CHAPTER TWO

Abraham, a Friend of God

Abraham was known as a friend of God because he knew how to build and maintain a relationship with God. God asked Abraham to leave his country and take a journey of faith with Him. Abraham obeyed the voice of God and left his country to journey with God.

James 2:23:

> And the scripture was fulfilled which saith, Abraham believed God, and it was imputed unto him for righteousness: and he was called the Friend of God.

Abraham took time to build his relationship with God. He listened to the Lord and was obedient to His voice. Abraham loved to build alters. Every encounter with God was accompanied by an altar where he worshipped and prayed to God. At times, God would come down and speak to Abraham, as a friend would speak to his friend. God made promises to Abraham and fulfilled every one of them.

Genesis 15:1-6:

> After these things the word of the Lord came to Abram in a vision, saying, Fear not Abram: I am thy shield and thy exceeding great reward.
>
> And Abram said, Lord God, what wilt thou give me, seeing I go childless, and the steward of my house is this Eliezer of Damascus?
>
> And Abram said, Behold, to me thou hast given no seed: and, lo, one born in my house is mine heir.
>
> And, behold, the word of the Lord came to him, saying, This shalt not be thine heir; but he that shall come forth out of thine own bowels shall be thine heir.
>
> And he brought him forth abroad, and said, Look now toward heaven, and tell the stars, if thou be able to number them: and he said unto him, So shall thy seed be.

> *And he believed in the Lord; and he counted it to him for righteousness.*

Abraham's relationship with God was so intimate that they were able to have heart-to-heart talks. God told Abraham that he was His exceeding reward, and Abraham responded as a friend talking to a friend and expressed his concern about his childlessness. He pointed out to God that his servant Eliezer was going to be his heir. God assured him that this would not happen because He would bless him with a child of his own and his seed would be so many, they would be numberless like the stars in the sky. Friends share what is on their hearts with each other. Abraham shared his heart with God about not having his own child to be his heir, and God shared that He was going to bless him with a child from whom would come innumerable descendants.

Genesis 17:1-9:

> *And when Abram was ninety years old and nine, the Lord appeared to Abram, and said unto him, I am the Almighty God; walk before me, and be thou perfect.*
>
> *And I will make my covenant between me and thee, and will multiply thee exceedingly.*

And Abram fell on his face: and God talked with him, saying,

As for me, behold, my covenant is with thee, and thou shalt be a father of many nations.

Neither shall thy name anymore be called Abram, but thy name shall be Abraham; for a father of many nations have I made thee.

And I will make thee exceedingly fruitful, and I will make many nations of thee, and kings shall come out of thee.

And I will establish my covenant between me and thee and thy seed after thee in their generations for an everlasting covenant, to be a God unto thee, and to thy seed after thee.

And I will give unto thee, and to thy seed after thee, the land wherein thou art a stranger, all the land of Canaan, for an everlasting possession; and I will be their God.

And God said unto Abraham, Thou shalt keep my covenant therefore, thou, and thy seed after thee in their generations.

God and Abraham started a friendship when Abraham was seventy-five years old. The friendship grew over the years, and when Abraham was ninety-nine years old, God appeared to him again and reaffirmed His love and friendship with him. God asked Abraham to walk before Him and be mature and then proceeded to take their relationship to a higher level by revealing His plan for Abraham's life. This included blessing him with many descendants, giving him and his descendants the land of Canaan as their possession, and establishing His covenant with Abraham and the generations that would follow him. When the Lord shared all these things with Abraham, Isaac was not on the scene as of yet, but the Lord knew his friend would believe what He told him. That is what friendship does; it builds confidence and trust. As our relationship with our Heavenly Father grows deeper, we will have a greater degree of confidence in His Word. Abraham and the Lord conversed often on the journey. Their frequent conversations caused the relationship to grow deeper and become more rewarding.

Genesis 18:17-18:

> *And the Lord said, shall I hide from Abraham that thing which I do;*
>
> *Seeing that Abraham shall surely become a great and mighty nation, and all the nations of the earth shall be blessed in him?*

Because of the relationship between God and Abraham, the Lord decided He could not hide from Abraham what He was going to do to Sodom. He knew He could depend on Abraham to lead his family in the way of truth. Therefore, God could trust Abraham and tell him what He was going to do to Sodom. Friends share their hearts with each other. They know what each other thinks in any given situation. Abraham lived up to God's expectation of him. When friends live up to each other's expectation, the relationship becomes more rewarding and fulfilling.

Genesis 19:29-30:

> And it came to pass, when God destroyed the cities of the plain, that God remembered Abraham, and sent Lot out of the midst of the overthrow, when he overthrew the cities in the which Lot dwelt.
>
> And Lot went up out of Zoar, and dwelt in the mountain, and his two daughters with him; for he feared to dwell in Zoar: and he dwelt in a cave, he and his two daughters.

Abraham's relationship with God not only benefited him but his nephew, Lot, who was spared from being destroyed with the inhabitants of Sodom because of Abraham. When we have a close relationship with God, our family members and relatives are blessed because of us. Therefore, when we are living in a close relationship with God, we are not living for ourselves alone, but others receive the benefits of that relationship too.

Genesis 22:1-10:

> *And it came to pass after these things, that God did tempt Abraham, and said unto him, Abraham; and he said, Behold, here I am.*
>
> *And he said, Take now thy son, thine only son Isaac, whom thou lovest, and get thee into the land of Moriah; and offer him there for a burnt offering upon one of the mountains which I will tell thee of.*
>
> *And Abraham rose up early in the morning, and saddled his ass, and took two of his young men with him, sand Isaac his son, and clave the wood for the burnt offering, and rose up, and went unto the place of which God had told him.*
>
> *Then on the third day Abraham lifted up his eyes, and saw the place afar off.*
>
> *And Abraham said unto his young men, Abide ye here with the ass; and I and the*

lad will go yonder and worship, and come again to you.

And Abraham took the wood of the burnt offering, and laid it upon Isaac his son: and he took the fire in his hand, and a knife; and they went both of them together.

And Isaac spoke unto Abraham his father, and said, My father: and he said, Here am I, my son. And he said, Behold the fire and the wood: but where is the lamb for a burnt offering?

And Abraham said, My son, God will provide himself a lamb for a burnt offering: so they went both of them together.

And they came to the place which God had told him of: and Abraham built an altar there, and bound Isaac his son, and laid him on the altar upon the wood.

And Abraham stretched forth his hand, and took the knife to slay his son.

As Abraham got to know his heavenly Father better, he was willing to do anything God asked of him. Because of his confidence in God, he knew he could trust God's words. Without hesitating, Abraham set out for Mount Moriah with his son and two servants. God had asked him to offer his son as a burnt offering, and he was going to be obedient. Abraham loved his son, but he loved his relationship with his heavenly Father much more. He knew the Lord would not lead him wrong.

As Abraham journeyed to the place, on the third day, he saw the location far off. He asked his two servants to wait where they were while he and Isaac would go, worship, and return. The servants could not go with them because they could not participate in Abraham's worship to his heavenly Father. Lovers love to relate to each other in private. They do not want the public involved because the public would not understand the nature of their relationship. As Abraham and Isaac journeyed, Isaac was concerned that the wood was ready and the fire was also ready but there was no lamb. His father reassured him that God would provide a lamb for the sacrifice. When Abraham arrived at Mount Moriah, he was ready to kill his son, but the angel of the Lord stopped him, assuring Abraham that he had passed the test in his willingness to sacrifice his son to please his heavenly Father. Friendship with God will prove itself at crucial times in our lives. Sincere friendship will manifest itself at important times of need.

Romans 4:17-21:

> *(As it is written, I have made thee a father of many nations) before him whom he believed, even God who quickeneth the dead, and calleth these things which be not as though they were.*
>
> *Who against hope believed in hope, that he might become the father of many nations, according to that which was spoken, So shall thy seed be.*
>
> *And being not weak in faith, he considered not his own body now dead, when he was about an hundred years old, neither yet the deadness of Sarah's womb*
>
> *He staggered not at the promise of God through unbelief; but was strong in faith, giving glory to God*
>
> *And being fully persuaded that, what he had promised, he was able also to perform.*

As Abraham and his heavenly Father continued to have strong friendship, Abraham was able to experience the supernatural power of God in his life. The Lord made a promise to make him a father of many nations when he was seventy-five years and did not have a child with Sarah. The promise of God did not manifest until he was one hundred years old and Sarah was ninety. Throughout those years of waiting on the promise, Abraham's faith in his Friend did not waver. He was fully persuaded that his Friend was able to deliver what He promised.

CHAPTER THREE

How to Build an Intimate Relationship with God

Prayer

What is prayer? Prayer is simply talking with God. Friends spend a lot of time talking to each other. They share what is on each other's heart. As Christians, we should adopt the style of Abraham to build altars to worship and talk to God. Prayer gives power, and our Father God has all the power. Therefore, if we spend quality time with Him in prayer and listen to His heartbeat for our lives, He will give us more power to carry out the assignments He gives to us.

Luke 11:2-13:

> *And he said unto them, When ye pray, say, Our Father which art in heaven, Hallowed*

be thy name. Thy kingdom come. Thy will be done, as in heaven, so in earth.

Give us day by day our daily bread.

And forgive us our sins; for we also forgive everyone that is indebted to us. And lead us not into temptation: but deliver us from evil.

And he said unto them, Which of you shall have a friend, and shall go unto him at midnight, and say unto him, Friend, lend me three loaves;

For a friend of mine in his journey is come to me, and I have nothing to set before him?

And he from within shall answer and say, Trouble me not: the door is now shut, and my children are with me in bed; I cannot rise and give thee.

I say unto you, Though he will not rise and give him, because he is his friend, yet because of his importunity he will rise and give him as many as he needeth.

And I say unto you, Ask, and it shall be given you; seek, and ye shall find; knock, and it shall be opened unto you.

For everyone that asketh receiveth; and he that seeketh findeth: and to him that knocketh it shall be opened.

If a son shall ask bread of any of you that is a father, will he give him a stone? or if he ask a fish, will he for a fish give him a serpent? or if he shall ask an egg, will he offer him a scorpion?

If ye then, being evil, know how to give good gifts unto your children: how much more shall your heavenly Father give the Holy Spirit to them that ask him.

Jesus came to earth as man. He knew that in order to carry out the will of the Father, He had to keep in close fellowship with Him. Prayer was a vital part of His life. He would spend all night in prayer, then He would spend the day ministering to the needs of the people. Through prayer, He was able to stay in close intimacy with His Father. When Jesus's disciples became interested in prayer, they asked Him to teach them how to pray. Jesus taught them the model prayer. He taught them to acknowledge God as their Father. This indicates there should be a relationship with Him. When we pray, we should be aware that His reign has come to earth and He wants His will to be done in the earth as it is in Heaven. We can talk to our Father about daily sustenance because, as a Father, He is concerned about our physical needs. When we follow the model prayer that Jesus taught His disciples, then we will be able to maintain an intimate relationship with the Father. Jesus taught us in the prayer to ask for His forgiveness and to forgive others just as He forgives us. Sin is the leading factor that destroys our relationship with the Father. However, we have an advocate in the person of Jesus Christ, God's Son, and we can approach the Father through Jesus and be cleansed from our sin.

Jesus used the analogy of friendship to teach the truth about persistence in prayer. He was showing His disciples that friends go the extra mile to help each other. If human beings will go the extra mile to help their friends, then when we have a relationship with the Father, He will do even more for us. Jesus also taught that earthly fathers know how to take care of their children. Therefore, our heavenly Father, Who is greater than our earthly fathers, will do even more for to demonstrate His great love for us.

As we give our lives to God and build a relationship with Him, we have the privilege to come to Him and ask according to His will, and He will answer us.

Obedience

Isaiah 1:19-20:

> *If ye be willing and obedient, ye shall eat the good of the land:*
>
> *But if ye refuse and rebel, ye shall be devoured with the sword: for the mouth of the Lord has spoken it.*

If we are willing to be obedient to our heavenly Father, our obedience will cause us to have a very good relationship with Him. However, if we refuse to be obedient, we will choose our own destruction. Our Father will not tolerate disobedient children. He is a loving Father, and He will discipline us in love.

Exodus 19:5-6:

> *Now therefore, if ye will obey my voice indeed, and keep my covenant, then ye shall be a peculiar treasure unto me above all people: for all the earth is mine:*
>
> *And ye shall be unto me a kingdom of priests, and an holy nation. These are the words which thou shalt speak unto the children of Israel.*

Obedience is vital to an intimate relationship with our heavenly Father. A good father will not tolerate disobedience in his children. If we are obedient, His whole heart belongs to us, for He is a Father who looks out for His children. He will protect us, and we will enjoy special favour from His hands.

Exodus 23:22:

> *But if thou shalt indeed obey his voice, and do all that I speak; then I will be an enemy unto thine enemies, and an adversary unto thine adversaries.*

Because we have a relationship with our heavenly Father, when the enemy comes against us, he will come against our Father too. When we have the heavenly Father on our side, we will always prevail over our enemies, for one with God is the majority.

Meditation

Spending time meditating on the Word of God helps us to build a relationship with our heavenly Father. Meditation is thinking on the Word of God. As our minds dwell on the Word of God, it is transferred to our spirit, and our daily life is transformed by it.

Psalm 1:1-2:

> *Blessed is the man that walketh not in the counsel of the ungodly, nor standeth in the way of sinners, nor sitteth in the seat of the scornful.*
>
> *But his delight is in the law of the Lord; and in his law doth he meditate day and night.*

The Word of God is like a love letter to His children. As we read and reread the Bible, it becomes part of our lives. The Word of God will cause our hearts to bond in a closer relationship with our heavenly Father.

Psalm 119:14-16:

> *I have rejoiced in the way of thy testimonies, as much as in all riches.*
>
> *I will meditate in the precepts, and have respect unto thy ways.*
>
> *I will delight myself in thy statutes: I will not forget thy word.*

When two persons are involved in a close relationship, it brings excitement. They will delight in each other and rejoice over each other's achievements.

They will develop trust in each other and please each other.

Joshua 1:8-9:

> *This book of the law shall not depart out of thy mouth: but thou shalt meditate therein day and night, that thou mayest observe to do according to all that is written therein: for then thou shalt make thy way prosperous, and then thou shalt have good success.*

Moses and the heavenly Father enjoyed a close relationship, and when the mantle was passed on to Joshua, he ensured that he too had a close relationship with the Lord. God gave Joshua some powerful promises and gave him the key to have a successful and prosperous life; He told Joshua prosperity and success would come as long as he stored the Word in his heart and lived by it.

Sacrifice

A sacrifice is something that is dear to us and that we are willing to give up so we may gain something better. When we have a close relationship with the Father, nothing is too good to give up for Him. Abraham was willing to sacrifice Isaac for a closer walk with the Father. A closer walk with the Father should be high on the Christian's agenda. We can sacrifice food to have a closer walk with the Father. For instance, fasting and spending time in prayer and meditating on the Word will bring us in a closer relationship with the Father. The greatest hindrance to relationships is selfishness. Sacrifice is an act of selflessness, and when we love the Lord, our entire life should be a sacrifice to Him.

Worship

Worship is expressing love to God. Whatever a person can do to express love to God is worship.

Genesis 22:5:

> *And Abraham said unto his young men, Abide ye here with the ass; and I and the lad will go yonder and worship, and come again to you.*

Abraham referred to sacrificing his son Isaac as worship. It was his way to express love to God. Other people express love in other ways.

Psalm 96:8-9"

> *Give unto the Lord the glory due unto his name: bring an offering, and come into his courts*

> *O worship the Lord in the beauty of holiness:*
> *fear before him, all the earth.*

As we gather each time in the house of God, our purpose should be to worship and glorify God. We worship Him in our giving of offerings, expressing our love to Him for blessing us with good health, strength, and the ability to work. We should worship Him by living holy lives; that is most precious to Him. He loves holiness, for He is a holy God.

John 4:23-24:

> *But the hour cometh, and now is, when the true worshippers shall worship the Father in spirit and in truth: for the Father seeketh such to worship him.*
>
> *God is a spirit: and they that worship him must worship him in spirit and in truth.*

Now is the time for us to worship God in spirit and in truth. The Holy Spirit will help us to worship God in spirit. It is time for us to fall prostrate before God and give Him all our praise, adoration, and worship.

CHAPTER FOUR

THE SECRET PLACE WITH GOD

Psalm 91:1-10:

> *He that dwelleth in the secret place of the most High shall abide under the shadow of the Almighty.*
>
> *I will say of the Lord, He is my refuge and my fortress: my God; in him will I trust.*
>
> *Surely he shall deliver thee from the snare of the fowler, and from the noisome pestilence.*
>
> *He shall cover thee with his feathers, and under his wings shalt thou trust: his truth shall be thy shield and buckler.*
>
> *Thou shalt not be afraid for the terror by night; nor for the arrow that flieth by day:*

Nor for the pestilence that walketh in darkness; nor for the destruction that wasteth at noonday.

A thousand shall fall at thy side, and ten thousand at thy right hand; but it shall not come nigh thee.

Only with thine eyes shalt thou behold and see the reward of the wicked.

Because thou hast made the Lord, which is my refuge, even the most High, thy habitation;

There shall no evil befall thee, neither shall any plague come nigh thy dwelling.

Lovers love to meet in secret places, for in secret places, they can express their heartbeat to each other. The more we love God, the more we want to be with Him in the secret place. Our heavenly Father loves us, and He provides safety for us in the secret place.

Persons who have a close relationship with God always make it a priority to find a secret place where they can be alone. In the secret place, they can have heart to heart talks with God, allowing the relationship to move to a higher level.

In the secret place, our lives will come under the influence and power of the Almighty. He will be a hiding place for us; He will be our stronghold. Our difficulties will not overwhelm us because we trust in Him. He will be a covering for our lives through the blood of Jesus. The Devil will not get to us or destroy us, for whatever the Devil does to us is what the Lord allows. God moved the hedge from around Job to allow the Devil to attack him, but God had confidence in Job that he would not let Him down.

Because we have made the decision to love the Lord, He will deliver us out of every situation. He will set us in a high and influential place and give us His favour. When we call on Him, He will answer us and bless us with long life.

Galatians 1:15-18:

> *But when it pleased God, who separated me from my mother's womb, and called me by his grace,*
>
> *To reveal his Son in me, that I might preach him among the heathen; immediately I conferred not with flesh and blood:*
>
> *Neither went I up to Jerusalem to them which were apostles before me; but I went into Arabia and returned again to Damascus.*

> *Then after three years I went up to Jerusalem to see Peter, and abode with him fifteen days.*

Paul was converted on the road to Damascus when he had an encounter with the Lord Jesus. He was knocked off his horse and blinded for three days. The spoke to him and commissioned him to preach the gospel. After his conversion, Paul headed for the desert of Arabia to spend some time alone with God. That was his secret place. There, he was able to develop a relationship with the heavenly Father. Those three years in a secret place with God set the stage for a great and successful ministry. Paul is known as one of the greatest apostles because of the revelations he received from God in the secret place. There, great ministries are conceived and brought to birth for God.

Genesis 32:24-28:

> *And Jacob was left alone; and there wrestled a man with him until the breaking of the day.*
>
> *And when he saw that he prevailed not against him, he touched the hollow of his thigh; and the hollow of Jacob's thigh was out of joint, as he wrestled with him.*

And he said, Let me go, for the day breaketh. And he said, I will not let thee go, except thou bless me.

And he said unto him, What is the name? And he said, Jacob.

And he said, Thy name shall be called no more Jacob, but Israel: for as a prince hast thou power with God and with men, and hast prevailed.

After Jacob had played all the tricks in the book, he realised he had to face reality. On his way back home, he realised he had to face his brother, Esau.

Jacob sent his family and servants ahead of him, and he stayed alone in a secret place with God. In that secret place, he had an encounter with God and became aware that he needed God. When we have an encounter with God in a secret place, we can never be the same. Jacob wrestled with God and refused to let go until he had received His blessing. His name was changed to Israel because he had prevailed with God and man. When we enter the secret place with God, we should stay there until we receive our breakthrough.

CHAPTER FIVE

KNOWING GOD IN A REAL WAY

Job 19:25-26:

> *For I know that my redeemer liveth, and that he shall stand at the latter day upon the earth.*
>
> *And though after my skin worms destroy this body, yet in my flesh shall I see God.*

Job knew God in a personal way. He did not have to ask somebody about God because he had built a close relationship with God. When the Devil made a serious attack on Job, he was unable to move Job from that close relationship with God. Job's attack was serious because the Devil used people who were close to him. The Devil killed his children and his livestock and used his friends to attack him. His wife advised him to curse God and die. If Job did not have an intimate relationship with God, he might have taken his wife's advice because what he experienced was enough to cause anyone to do just that.

Romans 8:35-39

> Who shall separate us from the love of Christ? shall tribulation, or distress, or persecution, or famine, or nakedness, or peril, or sword?
>
> As it is written for thy sake we are killed all the day long; we are accounted as sheep for the slaughter.
>
> Nay, in all these things we are more than conquerors through him that loved us.
>
> For I am persuaded, that neither death, nor life, nor angels, nor principalities, nor powers, nor things present, nor things to come,
>
> Nor height, nor depth, nor any other creature, shall be able to separate us from the love of God, which is in Christ Jesus our Lord.

When we know God in an intimate way and we experience adversities, God has a way of using what the Devil meant for harm to work out for our good and fulfil the purpose of God for our lives. Nothing that the Devil does has the ability to separate us from God's love. The relationship that we have with the Lord will enable us to rise above the attacks of the Enemy. They will be like water running off a duck's back. The Devil has the child of God on his hit list, but God will not allow him to be successful. The Lord will stop him in his tracks and cause the child of God to be more than a conqueror.

Philippians 3:10-14:

> *That I may know him and the power of his resurrection and the fellowship of his suffering being made conformable unto his death;*
>
> *If by any means I might attain unto the resurrection of the dead.*
>
> *Not as though I had already attained, either were already perfect: but I follow after, if that I may apprehend that for which also I am apprehended of Christ Jesus.*

One of Paul's greatest desires was to know God more. The more we know God, the more He will be available to work on our behalf. Paul wanted to Him much more because he wanted to experience His resurrection power in his life and in the lives of those he ministered unto. He wanted to share in his suffering. Fellowship brings intimacy. We should never be satisfied with our relationship with God because there is always more to know about Him. We should go after God with all our might. The writer of psalms forty-two compares his longing for God to a hart thirsty for water.

Psalm 42:1-2:

> As the hart panteth after the water brooks, so panteth my soul after thee o God.
>
> My soul thirsteth for God, for the living God: when shall I come and appear before God?

The strong desire for God caused Paul to forget those things which were behind; it gave him a hunger to press towards those things which were before him. Paul was able to have an outstanding relationship with the Father because he did not take his relationship with God lightly. He tried to be at his best with everything to enhance his relationship with the Father.

Psalm 46:10-11:

> Be still, and know that I am God: I will be exalted among the heathen, I will be exalted in the earth.

> *The Lord of hosts is with us; the God of Jacob is our refuge.*

To know God in an intimate way takes time. We have to learn to be quiet on the inside and outside in order to hear God perfectly. God speaks in a soft voice, so we have to listen carefully to Him and be willing to follow His instructions. The psalmist walked with God, and therefore, He was able to acknowledge God as his refuge and strength. He proved God in times of trouble; he was not afraid even when things seemed to be falling apart around him. His trust was in God.

2 Timothy 1:12:

> *For the which cause I also suffer these things: nevertheless I am not ashamed: for I know whom I have believed, and am persuaded that he is able to keep that which I have committed unto him against that day.*

A successful life is achieved from knowing God in a personal way, and Paul had that experience; therefore, he was not ashamed of the things he suffered for Christ. His relationship with God caused him to be fully persuaded that God would bring him through all the sufferings he experienced. When we are fully persuaded in God, the Devil has no power over us, for faith in God destroys the work of the Devil. Paul knew that his faith in God was bigger and stronger than any problem. Therefore, he was fully convinced that the God he served would take care of him in any situation.

Matthew 7:22-26:

> *Many will say to me in that day, Lord, Lord, have we not prophesied thy name? And in thy name have cast out devils? And in thy name have done many wonderful works?*
>
> *And then will I profess unto them, I never knew you: depart from me , ye that work iniquity.*
>
> *Therefore whosoever heareth these sayings of mine, and doeth them, I will liken him unto a wise man, which built his house upon a rock:*
>
> *And the rain descended, and the floods came, and the winds blew, and beat upon that house; and it fell not: for it was founded upon a rock.*
>
> *And everyone that heareth these sayings of mine, and doeth them not, shall be likened unto a foolish man, who built his house upon the sand.*

There are people who are heavily involved in the work of God and do not have a relationship with God. They may seek to impress someone, but it will be very sad for them on that final day, for the Lord will tell them He doesn't know them and never did, and they will be banished from His presence.

God is concerned that every Christian have a relationship with Him so we can know the will of God for our lives. God has an assignment for each of us, and it is only when we have a relationship with Him that we can know that assignment and fulfill it. God considers people who hear His Word and do so as wise people. They are building a life that will last and stand the test of time. When we have a close relationship with God, we will receive greater revelation from His Word. Those who do not obey His Word are called "fools." It is the Word that helps us to build a relationship with God. If the Word of God is not in us, then there is no relationship with God. Therefore, when the storms of life come, they will have disastrous effects on those whose lives are not grounded in His Word.

CHAPTER SIX

---◇---

An Intimate Walk with God Produces Fruit

Genesis 5:22-24:

> *And Enoch walked with God after he begat Methuselah three hundred years, and begat sons and daughters.*
>
> *And all the days of Enoch were three hundred sixty and five years:*
>
> *And Enoch walked with God: and he was not; for God took him.*

An intimate walk with God, as referred to in the above verses, is a lifestyle. Enoch's lifestyle was pleasing to God. He had an intimate relationship with God, and he allowed his relationship with God to influence every aspect of his life. Enoch and God had a very close friendship. He did not allow anything to come between him and God.

They were so close that one day, as they were walking and having rich fellowship, God took him from the earth so they could continue the fellowship

In the Christian life, each of us is responsible for our own walk with God; no one should have to teach us how to walk with God. If we are in a relationship with God, His Holy Spirit will guide and direct us in our walk with God.

Deuteronomy 5:32-33:

> *Ye shall observe to do therefore as the Lord your God has commanded you: ye shall not turn aside to the right hand or to the left.*
>
> *Ye shall walk in all the ways which, the Lord your God has commanded you, that ye may live, and that it may be well with you, and that ye may prolong your days in the land which ye shall possess.*

The children of Israel were God's chosen people. God loved them even though they failed Him so many times in their walk with Him. He wanted the best for them and brought them out of Egypt and into a good land, a land of plenty. However, God wanted them to be thankful and not take His blessings for granted. The Word of the Lord to them was that they must pay close attention to His Word. They were not to turn to the right nor the left, but to conduct themselves according to His Word. If they were obedient to His Word, they would enjoy a good life and things would go well with them in the land He had given them.

Micah 6:8:

> *He hath showed thee, O man, what is good: and what doth the Lord require of thee, but to do justly, and to love mercy, and to walk humbly with thy God?*

In walking intimately with God, there are some things required of us. We must be just, we must be merciful, and we must walk humbly before God. God is a God of justice and mercy, and when we walk with Him in an intimate way, these attributes will be manifested in our lives.

Ephesians 5:14-17:

> *Wherefore he saith, Awake thou that sleepest, and arise from the dead, and Christ shall give thee light.*
>
> *See then that ye walk circumspectly, not as fools, but as wise,*
>
> *Redeeming the time, because the days are evil.*
>
> *Wherefore be ye not unwise, but understanding what the will of the Lord is.*

We should not allow the Devil to lead us to sleep spiritually and become dead in our spiritual walk with God. God wants us to be wide awake as we walk on our Christian journeys, walking circumspectly and not allowing our lives to be contaminated with sin. We should walk with the understanding that we know the will of God, which is to be holy as He is holy. We have to be wise spiritually so we can be a step ahead of the Devil. When we are a step ahead of him, he will not have anything over us. As we stay alert and walk in the light in these evil times, we are able to use our time wisely and be productive for the kingdom of God.

John 8:12:

> *Then spake Jesus again unto them, saying, I am the light of the world: he that followeth me shall not walk in darkness, but shall have the light of life.*

Jesus and the Word of God are one. To follow Jesus is to follow the Word of God. The Word of God brings light to our lives. The light of God's Word shines in our life and causes us to be fruitful in our walk with Him.

1 John 1:7:

> *But if we walk in the light, as he is in the light, we have fellowship one with another, and*

the blood of Jesus Christ his son cleanseth us from all sin.

God is light, and there is no darkness in Him. As we walk in the light of His Word, we are able to relate to one another, and people will see that God has done something in our lives because they reflect the change God has done in us. The light we walk in will also cause us to produce fruit unto holiness. As light plays an important part in plant life, allowing them to make food and reproduce, similarly, the light that we walk in as Christians will also cause us to bear fruit because that is what God expects of us.

John 15:1-8:

> *I am the vine and my father is the husbandman.*
>
> *Every branch in me that beareth not fruit he taketh away and every branch that beareth fruit he purgeth it, that it may bring forth more fruit.*
>
> *Now ye are clean through the word which I have spoken unto you,*
>
> *Abide in me and I in you, as the branch cannot bear fruit of itself, except it abide*

in the vine, no more can ye, except ye abide in me,

I am the vine, ye are the branches: He that abide in me. And I in him, the same bringeth forth much fruit; for without me ye can do nothing.

If a man abide not in me, he is cast forth as a branch, and is withered; and men gather them, and cast them into the fire, and they are burned.

If ye abide in me and my words abide in you, ye shall ask what ye will, and it shall be done unto you.

Herein is my father glorified, that ye bear much fruit; so shall ye be my disciples.

Jesus stressed the importance of abiding in Him because without Him, we can do nothing. Bearing fruit is indicative of an intimate walk with God. In the natural when a man and a woman become intimate with each other and build a relationship, they eventually get married. This leads to a sexual relationship, and from that sexual relationship, children are produced. The children carry the characteristics of the parents and resemble them in appearance. In the spiritual when we become intimate with God, we start receiving God's nature. As we receive God's nature, our lives become productive in spiritual things. We are the branches that project from God. To be fruitful, we have to abide in the Word. To abide in the Word is to abide in God. The branch can only produce fruit from the life of God. The branch that is not fruitful is taken away for wasting God's time.

God is glorified when our lives are productive. Productivity is indicative that the life of God is working in and through us. God calls us His friends and not servants. Friends have a relationship, but servants come and do their duty and leave. Friends share their hearts with each other.

Acts 2:1-2:

> *And when the day of Pentecost was fully come, they were all with one accord in one place.*
>
> *And suddenly there came a sound from heaven as of a rushing mighty wind, and it filled all the house where they were sitting.*

Before He ascended to His Father, Jesus instructed the disciples to wait for the promise of the Father in the person of the Holy Ghost. They were to continue His ministry, and He knew they would not be able to do so without the power of the Holy Ghost in their lives. They needed the Holy Ghost if they were going to have productive ministries. The Holy Ghost came as Jesus promised, and they were all filled; all 120 were filled with the Holy Ghost.

The disciples were able to do mighty works for Jesus. As they preached the Word, the Lord gave His confirmation with signs and wonders.

Acts 5:12-14:

> *And by the hands of the apostles were many signs and wonders wrought among the people; (and they were all with one accord in Solomon's porch.*
>
> *And of the rest durst no man join himself to them: but the people magnified them.*
>
> *And believers were the more added to the Lord, multitudes both of men and women.)*

Through the power of the Holy Ghost, multitudes came to know Jesus as Lord and Saviour of their lives. The disciples were used mightily, and the Lord was glorified. However, the Enemy did not like what was happening, and the church was persecuted for preaching in Jesus's name. King Herod killed James, the brother of John, and proceeded to do the same to Peter.

Acts 12:5-10:

Peter therefore was kept in prison: but prayer was made without ceasing of the church unto God for him.

And when Herod would have brought him forth, the same night Peter was sleeping between two soldiers, bound with two chains: and the keepers before the door kept the prison.

And, behold, the angel of the Lord came upon him, and a light shined in the prison: and he smote peter on the side, and raised him up, saying, Arise up quickly. And his chains fell off from his hands.

And the angel said unto him gird thyself, and bind on thy sandals. And so he did. And he saith unto him, Cast thy garment about thee and follow me;

And he went out, and followed him; and wist not that it was true which was done by the angel; but thought he saw a vision.

When they were past the first and the second ward, they came unto the iron gate

> that leadeth unto the city; which opened to them of his own accord: and they went out, and passed through one street; and forthwith the angel departed from him.

The prayer of the saints released the angel from Heaven who came to Peter's rescue. Peter was chained between two soldiers, and there were soldiers at the door of the prison. That was maximum security; however, security could not keep the angel of God out of the cell, and Peter was released without the keepers' knowledge. When prayers are being uttered by the people of God who have an intimate relationship with the Lord, the Devil and his forces will be in trouble. Peter was released to go and do the work of the Lord.

Daniel 11:32:

> And such as do wickedly against the covenant shall he corrupt by flatteries: but the people that do know their God shall be strong and do exploits.

Those who disobey the Word of God shall become corrupt and their path will be full of sorrow. However, those who know God shall be strong and do great things for God. They shall be blessed in every area of their lives and shall be a blessing to others. This is the product of an intimate relationship with the Father.

CHAPTER SEVEN

THE INTIMACY OF JESUS AND HIS FATHER

Luke 2:40, 49

> *And the child grew, and waxed strong in spirit, filled with wisdom: and the grace of God was upon him.*
>
> *And he said unto them, How is it that ye sought me? Wist ye not that I must be about my Father's business?*

Jesus came to earth as a man to express the Father's love to man. Jesus kept in close contact with His Father. From a child, He grew strong in spirit, and godly wisdom was in Him. When His parents took Him to Jerusalem, on the returning journey, they realised that Jesus was missing. He could not be found amongst their relatives and friends, and they had to go back to Jerusalem to search for Him. They found Him in the temple in the midst of doctors and lawyers, both listening to them and asking them questions. Those who heard Him were amazed at His understanding, and when His parents found Him, they told Him they were searching for Him for three days. He responded by asking them if they did not know that He had to be about His Father's business. At an early age, He knew what His mission was and that His relationship with His Father was very important.

Matthew 3:16-17:

> *And Jesus, when he was baptized, went up straightway out of the water: and, lo, the heavens were opened unto him, and he saw the spirit of God descending like a dove, and lighting upon him:*
>
> *And lo a voice from heaven, saying, This is my beloved Son, in whom I am well pleased.*

Jesus is our perfect example of how to build a relationship with the Father. Jesus always focused on the will of His Father. He was not distracted by anything. When Jesus was baptized, He gave us an example of what we should do with our lives. The Father expressed His pleasure with His Son as He sent the Holy Spirit to Him to empower Him to fulfill His earthly mission.

Matthew 4:1-4:

> *Then was Jesus led up of the Spirit into the wilderness to be tempted of the devil.*
>
> *And when he had fasted forty days and forty nights, he was afterward an hungred.*
>
> *And when the tempter came to him, he said, If thou be the Son of God, command that these stones be made bread.*
>
> *But he answered and said. It is written, Man shall not live by bread alone, but by every word that proceedeth out of the mouth of God.*

The Devil will always seek to test our relationship with the Father. Jesus was thirty years, and during those years, He had a committed relationship with the Father. The Devil was trying to destroy that relationship just as he did with Adam and Eve in the garden.

Jesus was led by the Spirit into the wilderness where He fasted for forty days and forty nights. He was getting rid of anything, including selfishness, that would try to raise its ugly head in Him to prevent Him from doing the will of God. When the Devil came to tempt Jesus to prove His sonship with the Father, the Devil failed. He also tried to tempt Jesus with pride. It was not Jesus's time to do miracles. If He had done what the Devil wanted, He would have jeopardised His relationship with the Father and failed in His mission to save us from our sins.

Jesus did not come to prove anything to the Devil. He came to do the Father's will. He used the Word of God and the sword of the Spirit, and the Devil had to leave Him. Jesus was steadfast and focused, and His relationship with the Father was the most important thing to Him. He was not going to let the Devil destroy that relationship. After His victory over the Devil, angels came and ministered unto Him.

Matthew 11:25-28:

> *At that time Jesus answered and said, I thank thee ,O Father, Lord of heaven and earth, , because thou hast hid these things from the wise and prudent, and hast revealed them unto babes.*
>
> *Even so, Father, for so it seemed good in thy sight.*
>
> *All things are delivered unto me of my Father: and no man knoweth the Son, but the Father, neither knoweth any man the*

> *Father, save the Son, and he to whomsoever the Son will reveal him.*
>
> *Come unto me, all ye that labour and are heavy laden, and I will give you rest.*

Jesus started His ministry teaching. Preaching and healing the sick. Jesus was able to minister to the people because of His relationship with His Father. Jesus thanked His Father for revealing truth to those who had childlike faith and not to those who thought they were wise in their own eyes. Those with childlike faith have a relationship with the Father because they know that they cannot depend on themselves, for without the Father, they are nothing. Jesus told His audience that the Father had delivered all things to him. He informed them that no one can know the Father without His help, and no one can know Him without the Father's help. This was the nature of the relationship between Him and His Father.

John 8:16-19:

> *And yet if I judge, my judgement is true: for I am not alone, but I and then father that sent me.*
>
> *It is also written in your law, that the testimony of two men is true.*

> *I am one that bear witness of myself, and the Father that sent me beareth witness of me. Then said they unto him, Where is your Father? Jesus answered, ye neither know me, nor my father: if ye had known me, ye should have known my Father also.*

During His ministry, Jesus always pointed people to His Father. He was on His Father's business, and it was important that He let the people know that. It was also important to let them know that He and His Father were one. Jesus's relationship with His Father was so important that He would spend all night in prayer communicating with the Father. This empowered Him to carry out the mission of His Father during the day. We can learn from the relationship Jesus had with His father while He was on earth because all of us who accepted Jesus are His children. God wants us to have that same intimate relationship with Him.

CHAPTER EIGHT

INTIMACY BETWEEN GOD AND MOSES

Exodus 2:1-4:

> And there went a man of the house of Levi, and took to wife a daughter of Levi.
>
> And the woman conceived, and bare a son: and when she saw him that he was a goodly child, she hid him three months.
>
> And when she could no longer hide him, she took for him an ark of bulrushes, and daubed it with slime and with pitch, and put the child therein; and she laid it in the flags by the river's bank
>
> And his sister stood afar off, to wit what would be done to him. Moses was born in a time when Pharaoh was killing all the male children in Israel.

When Moses was born, his mother saw there was something special about him and hid him for three months. When she could no longer hide him, she released him into the hand of God by putting him in a homemade boat and placing it in the Nile. Pharaoh's daughter eventually found him, and with the help of Moses's sister Miriam, Moses was handed back to his mother to care for him.

When Moses became a man, he knew that he was not an Egyptian, but an Israelite. He realised that he had a special assignment, and one day, as he went to visit his brethren, he killed an Egyptian who was mistreating his fellow Israelite. On another occasion, as he went out to visit his brethren, he saw two of them fighting and tried to intervene. The one who was in the wrong asked Moses if he wanted to kill him as he did the Egyptian. Moses realised his crime was not a secret and decided to flee Egypt to get away from Pharaoh's wrath.

God led him into the wilderness, and there he became a member of Jethro's family in Midian, taking care of sheep. One day, he noticed a strange sight. A bush was on fire, but it was not being consumed by the flames. As he drew closer, God spoke to him and told him He was going to send him back to Egypt to Pharaoh to tell him to let His people go. That was the beginning of Moses's relationship with God. Moses presented God with all the excuses he could think of. He was not eloquent; the people would not believe him; who should he tell them sent him? And, eventually, he told God to send someone else.

However, Moses could not get away from the plan of God, and he went to Egypt to free the Israelites.

Exodus 6:1-5:

> *Then the Lord said unto Moses, now shalt thou see what I will do to Pharaoh: for with a strong hand will he let them go, and with a strong hand shall he drive them out of his land.*
>
> *And God spake unto Moses, and said unto him, I am the Lord:*
>
> *And I appeared unto Abraham, unto Isaac, and unto Jacob, by the name of God Almighty, but by my name JEHOVAH was I not known to them.*
>
> *And I have also established my covenant with them, to give them the land of Canaan, the land of their pilgrimage, wherein they were strangers.*
>
> *And I have also heard the groaning of the children of Israel, whom the Egyptians*

> keep in bondage; and I have remembered my covenant.

God does not go back on His word. Because of Moses's relationship with the Lord, he was able to answer the call of God to go to Egypt and bring God's people out. On the way to the promise land, there were many tests. Many times, God wanted to destroy the people and raise up a new nation. However, Moses interceded for them, and God listened to Moses and spared them. Because of Moses's relationship with God, God was able to give him instructions on what to do when any difficult situation arose. He was willing to do what God asked him to do. That contributed greatly to their relationship. God loves people who are obedient and follow His instructions.

Exodus 19:3-6:

> And Moses went up unto God, and the Lord called unto him out of the mountain saying, Thus shalt thou say to the house of Jacob and tell the children of Israel;

> Ye have seen what I did unto the Egyptians, and how I bare you on eagles' wings, and brought you unto myself.

> Now therefore if ye will obey my voice in deed and keep my covenant, then ye shall

> *be a peculiar treasure unto me above all people: for all the earth is mine.*
>
> *And ye shall be unto me a kingdom of priests, and an holy nation. These are the words which thou shalt speak unto the children of Israel.*

When two persons are building an intimate relationship, they will meet often and have heart-to-heart talks. This enables each person to know what is on the others mind. This was the case with God and Moses. They would meet, and God would share His plans for the children of Israel with Moses. Moses was able to know the ways of God because of his relationship with God. The children of Israel were able to see the power of God through Moses's relationship with Him.

After the children of Israel came out of Egypt, God was close to them. He went before them in a pillar of cloud by day and a pillar of fire by night. God did not bring them out of Egypt and abandon them. He was available for them to ensure that they were safe all the way to the promised land. God reminded them how much they meant to Him and that they were His treasure.

God shared His heart with Moses, and Moses shared God's heart with the people. Whenever people make God's people their enemy, then they become God's enemy.

Exodus 24:15-18:

> *And Moses went up into the mount, and a cloud covered the mount.*
>
> *And the glory of the Lord abode upon mount Sinai, and the cloud covered it six days: and the seventh day he called unto Moses out of the midst of the cloud.*
>
> *And the sight of the glory of the Lord was like devouring fire on the top of the mount in the eyes of the children of Israel.*
>
> *And Moses went into the midst of the cloud, and gat him up into the mount: and Moses was in the mount forty days and forty nights.*

God called Moses to Mount Sinai, and the mount was covered by a cloud and the glory of the Lord. It was the time when God was going to deliver the ten commandments to Moses. In the presence of God, there is no need for anything else. His relationship with God enabled Moses to stay on the mount for forty days and forty nights. God's friendship is a sustaining force. When we are in the presence of God, everything else pales in the light of God's glory and grace.

CHAPTER NINE

LIVING IN THE PRESENCE OF GOD

Living in the presence of God and enjoying His friendship are the greatest things that can happen in a person's life. Each Christian should seek to live in the presence of God. Our relationship with God should cause us to live at the highest standard, then our lives will be outstanding and rewarding.

Exodus 34-35:

> *And the children of Israel saw the face of Moses, that the skin of Moses' face shone: and Moses put the veil upon his face again, until he went in to speak with him.*
>
> *When Moses came down from mount Sinai his face shone and the children of Israel and Aaron were afraid to come near to him. The presence of God caused his face to shine*

> and he had to put a veil over his faced as
> he talked to the people.

Exodus 33:14-15:

> And he said, My presence shall go with thee,
> and I will give thee rest.
>
> And he said unto him, if thy presence go not
> with me, carry us not up hence.

The presence of God helps us enjoy intimacy with God. The presence of God gives us the assurance of God's love. His presence gives us strength for the Christian journey. Without the presence of God, life can become difficult and turbulent.

Moses was aware of the importance of the presence of God. Moses realised leading the children of Israel was a great task, and he told the Lord he wanted His presence with him. Moses told the Lord if His presence did not go with them, he must not take them further. God reassured Moses that His presence would be with them. He would go with them all the way.

1 Chronicles 16:27-29:

> Glory and honour are in his presence:
> strength and gladness are in his place

Give unto the Lord ye kindreds of the people, give unto the Lord glory and strength.

Give unto the Lord the glory due unto his name: bring an offering, and come before him: worship the Lord in the beauty of holiness.

When God's presence is embraced and encouraged to manifest in our lives and we come together in the Lord's house, then His glory will be manifested among us. His name will be honoured, and people will leave the house of God blessed because of His presence. The presence of God gives strength physically, emotionally, and spiritually. God is glorified when Christians live in His presence. Christians are the carriers of the presence of God. As we carry the presence of God in our jobs, God is glorified and people are attracted to God. We should carry His presence in the marketplace and everywhere we go, so the name of the Lord be magnified.

Psalm 16:11:

Thou wilt show me the path of life: in thy presence is fulness of joy, at thy right hand there are pleasures for evermore.

When we are intimate with God, He gets what belongs to Him from our lives. We will fear and respect and revere

Him. We will live holy lives, for holiness is a vital part of an intimate relationship with God. Without holiness, we cannot see God. We cannot have an intimate relationship with Him if we are not living holy. In God's presence, we have joy. His presence causes our lives to be stable; our lives will not be up and down like a yo-yo. We will grow in the grace of God, and His presence in us will impact the lives of others and make them better people. They will see the joy of the Lord in our lives. *The joy of the Lord is our strength.* His presence will give us pleasure and the Christian life will be joyous and rewarding. Even when we are experiencing trial and persecution, they will not rob us of our joy.

Psalm 31:20:

> *Thou shalt hide them in the secret of thy presence from the pride of man: thou shalt keep them secretly in a pavilion from the strife of tongues.*

The presence of God forms a hedge of protection for our lives from the attacks of the Devil. His presence is a hiding place for our lives. We are secure and well-protected and preserved. When a child is by his father, he feels secure from all harm. As a hen covers her chicks, so our heavenly Father covers His children. He takes us in His arms and cherishes us with His love.

Psalm 100:1-5:

Make a joyful noise unto the Lord, all ye lands.

Serve the Lord with gladness: come before his presence with singing.

Know ye that the Lord he is God: it is he that hath made us, and not we ourselves; we are his people, and the sheep of his pasture.

Enter into his gates with thanksgiving, and into his courts with praise: be thankful unto him, and bless his name.

For the Lord is good; his mercy is everlasting; and his truth endureth to all generations.

Our heavenly Father is God of life. As we connect with Him, He gives us life. Jesus came so that we might have life in abundance. It is a pleasure to serve the Lord, and we should reflect that pleasure in our appearance. When people look at us, they should see that something great has taken place in our lives. We should enter into the place of worship with thankful hearts. We have the Almighty God as our Father, and He has our best intertest at heart. Praise and worship should be part of our lifestyle to express to our Father how much we love Him. He is good and has shown His goodness in an awesome way.

CHAPTER TEN

BE FLEXIBLE IN THE HAND OF GOD

As children of God, we should have the desire to build a relationship with God. If we want to have a dynamic relationship with God, it is important that we learn to be flexible in the hand of God. He may ask us to go certain places at certain times. If our hearts are not sensitive to the voice of God, we can miss Him.

Jonah 1:1-4:

> *Now the word of the Lord came unto Jonah the son of Amittai, saying,*
>
> *Arise, and go to Nineveh, that great city, and cry against it; for their wickedness is come up before me.*
>
> *But Jonah rose up to flee unto Tarshish from the presence of the Lord, and went down to*

> Joppa; and he found a ship going to Tarshish: so he paid the fare thereof, and went down into it, to go with them unto Tarshish from the presence of the Lord.
>
> But the Lord sent out a great wind into the sea, and there was a mighty tempest in the sea, so that the ship was like to be broken.

Jonah had a relationship with God, but he was not flexible in the hand of God; he wanted to do as he liked. When we have a relationship with God and want to do things our own way, we cause conflict with the purposes of God for our lives. The will of God for Jonah was to go to Nineveh and deliver God's message to the nation. Jonah was not flexible in the hand of God, and because of that, he got himself in trouble with God. He made the mistake of believing he could run away from God, forgetting that God is the Creator of everything. He ended up in the belly of a fish.

Jonah 2:1-2, 10:

> Then Jonah prayed unto the Lord his God out of the fish's belly,
>
> And said, I cried by reason of mine affliction unto the Lord, and he heard me;

out of the belly of hell cried I, and thou heardest my voice.

And the Lord spake unto the fish, and it vomited out Jonah upon the dry land.

Jonah was able to learn important lessons in the belly of the fish. First, he learned he should have obeyed God and sought to fulfill His will. Secondly, he realised that he could not run away from the presence of God. When Jonah looked to God in prayer, he received help. The Lord caused the fish to vomit him on the seashore. After that experience, Jonah learned his lessons, and he was ready to follow God. A journey that would have taken three days was done in one day. God knows how to teach us to remember Him and be obedient to His purpose for our lives. God will allow us to go through some bad experiences, not to kill us, but to make us flexible in His hands. There are times we allow ourselves to be distracted from the purpose of God, and God has to teach us a lesson to make us flexible, willing, and obedient.

After the experience in the belly of the fish, Jonah went and preached the message to the people of Nineveh. Now, Jonah was willing to work with God and walk with God and not go his own way. The people received the message and repented, turning from their wicked ways. If Jonah had only flowed with God, life would have been much better for him. Similarly, we can make life much better for us if we flow with God, do what He says, and resist doing our own thing. The people of Nineveh were able to make things right with God because Jonah went and gave them the message.

There are many people today who are missing God's message because they are not willing to be flexible. Consequently, many are on their way to Hell and need someone to share with them the message of salvation. When we are flexible in the hands of God, He is able to use us to accomplish great works in His kingdom.

Moses was a person who was flexible in the hands of God. Therefore, God was able to do great things with him.

Genesis 12:1, 4:

> *Now the lord had said unto Abraham, Get thee out of thy country, and from thy kindred, and from thy father's house, unto a land that I will shew thee:*
>
> *So Abram departed, as the Lord had spoken unto him and Lot went with him: and Abram was seventy and five years old when he departed out of Haran.*

Abram was a man who was flexible in the hand of God. He flowed with the plan and purpose of God for his life.

Abram was so flexible that when God asked him to uproot himself from his country, his relatives, and his home at the age of seventy-five, he obeyed. That was a major change in his life, but he was flexible enough to believe God. He did not put up any resistance but took God at His word and obeyed, not knowing where he was going.

Abram was flexible also in obeying God when He asked him to sacrifice Isaac. This was the son that God had promised He would use to make Abram's descendants innumerable. However, Abraham rose to the occasion and obeyed God. As we become older, we have the tendency to become set in our ways and are not open to change. Abraham was not like that. God is still looking for people with a level of commitment and flexibility like Abraham. When God finds people like that, He does not hesitate to use them for His glory and honour.

CHAPTER ELEVEN

———⋈———

The Holy Spirit and Intimacy

The Holy Spirit is the One who will help us build an intimate relationship with the Lord.

John 14:15-10:

> *If ye love me, keep my commandments.*
>
> *And I will pray the Father, and he shall give you another Comforter, that he may abide with you for ever;*
>
> *Even the Spirit of truth; whom the world cannot receive, because it seeth him not, neither knoweth him: for he dwelleth with you, and shall be in you.*
>
> *I will not leave you comfortless: I will come to you.*

> *Yet a little while, and the world seeth me no more; but ye see me: because I live, ye shall live also.*

The Holy Spirit was sent to be alongside us to help us do the will of God. Without the Holy Spirit, we are unable to fulfill the will of God. After Jesus had finished His earthly ministry, He told His disciples to wait at Jerusalem until they were endued with the power of the Holy Spirit. Jesus knew that without the Holy Spirit, the disciples would fail. The Holy Spirit is the Spirit of truth. He will lead us in the truth. The Holy Spirit will reveal the Father to us and teach us how to build a relationship with the Father.

John 14:26:

> *But the Comforter, which is the Holy Ghost, whom the Father will send in my name, he shall teach you all things, and bring all things to your remembrance, whatsoever I have said unto you.*

The Holy Spirit has all the attributes of the Father that the church needs. The Holy Spirit is the Comforter from the Father. When we are in trouble, He is able to give us words of comfort that enables us to make it through our troubles safely. The Holy Spirit will teach us and bring all things to our remembrance. He is the Engineer of the

Word of God; holy men of God spoke as they were led by the Holy Ghost.

Psalm 25:4-5:

> Shew me thy ways, O Lord; teach me thy paths.
>
> Lead me in thy truth, and teach me: for thou art the God of my salvation; on thee do I wait all the day.

God is light, and there is no darkness in Him. He wants His children to walk in the light. The Holy Spirit brings light to our spirit from His Word. The psalmist asked God to teach him and show him the paths God wanted him to travel on.

Acts 6

> Wherefore, brethren, look ye out among you seven men of honest report, full of the Holy Ghost and wisdom, whom we may appoint over this business.

When the early church was growing at a rapid rate, the disciples needed people to help in the ministry of taking care of the widows. Being full of the Holy Ghost was one of the requirements those chosen had to meet. Stephen was one of those who were chosen because he met the requirements. He did great wonders and miracles among the people.

Some leaders of the synagogue saw Stephen as a threat and rose up against him. They disputed with him but were unable to resist his wisdom because of the power of the Holy Ghost that was at work in him. They accused him of speaking blasphemous words against Moses and God. The high priest gave him a chance to speak before his accusers. He spoke under the anointing of the Holy Ghost. He reminded them of the children of Israel in Egypt, how Moses led them out, and their rebellion against Moses and God in the wilderness. He did not spare his words, and they were convicted by his words. In retaliation, they stoned him to death. Stephen asked God to forgive them as he breathed his last breath. Stephen was able to speak so convincingly because of the power of the Holy Ghost in his life and relationship with God. The power of the Holy Ghost is not only for the good times but the bad times also. When we face bad times, the Holy Ghost shows up in a greater way.

Acts 20:22-24:

> *And now, behold, I go bound in the spirit unto Jerusalem, not knowing the things that shall befall me there:*

> *Save that the Holy Ghost witnesseth in every city, saying that bonds and afflictions abide me.*
>
> *But none of these things move me, neither count I my life dear unto myself, so that I might finish my course with joy, and the ministry, which I have received of the Lord Jesus, to testify the gospel of the grace of God.*

Paul experienced great afflictions, but he was able to endure them successfully because the power of the Holy Ghost resided in him. He was not afraid to face difficulties head on and be victorious. He was headed for Jerusalem, knowing persecution awaited him there. He was determined that nothing would deter him from going where God wanted him to go and fulfilling the ministry God gave to him. Paul was sold out to the Lord, and his relationship with the Lord—with the help of the Holy Ghost—gave him the confidence that everything would be alright.

Acts 8:29-31:

> *Then the Spirit said unto Philip, Go near, and join thyself to this chariot.*

> *And Philip ran thither to him, and heard him read the prophet Esaias, and said, Understandest thou what thou readest?*
>
> *And he said, How can I, except some man should guide me? And he desired Philip that he would come up and sit with him.*

Philip allowed the Holy Spirit to guide him. The Ethiopian eunuch was returning home from Jerusalem and was reading from the prophet Isaiah. The Spirit of the Lord led Philip to go and sit with him. Philip was able to explain the scripture to him. The Ethiopian received the Word and accepted Jesus in his heart. Straightaway, he requested water baptism which Philip did for him.

When they came up out of the water, the Holy Spirit took Philip away, and the eunuch went on his way, rejoicing. The Holy Spirit is so vital in our relationship with the heavenly Father. He makes all the difference in that relationship.

CHAPTER TWELVE

THE INCREASE OF THE ANOINTING

Our heavenly Father does not want us to stay in one place in Him. He wants us to experience as much as we can in Him. His intention is to change us from one stage of glory to another. He wants His anointing grace to increase in our lives.

1 Peter 2:1-5:

> *Wherefore laying aside all malice, and all guile, and hypocrisies, and envies, and all evil speakings,*
>
> *As newborn babes, desire the sincere milk of the word, that ye may grow thereby.*
>
> *If so be ye have tasted that the Lord is gracious.*

> *To whom coming as unto a living stone, disallowed indeed of men, but chosen of God and precious*
>
> *Ye also as lively stones, are built up a spiritual house, an holy priesthood, to offer up spiritual sacrifices, acceptable to God by Jesus Christ.*

The anointing increases on the life of believers when we give ourselves to studying the Word and spending quality time in prayer and fasting. Additionally, we have to put aside anything that will hinder the flow of the anointing. Malice, hypocrisy, envy, and evil speaking are all works of the flesh and should have no place in the life of the child of God. We should have a strong desire for God. They that hunger and thirst after righteousness shall be filled. Every achievement begins with a desire to achieve. A greater anointing from God's Spirit begins with a strong desire for the Holy Spirit that the anointing can increase in our lives. Our desire for more of the anointing should be a sincere one, not based on selfish motives or ambition. God wants us to be a holy temple for the Holy Ghost to express His will here on earth.

2 Peter 3:18:

> *But grow in grace, and in the knowledge of our Lord and Saviour Jesus Christ. To him be glory both now and forever. Amen.*

To increase in the anointing is to grow in grace and in the knowledge of God. Many Christians want to flow in the power of the Holy Ghost yet have no knowledge of the Word.

Psalm 23:5-6:

> *Thou preparest a table before me in the presence of my enemies: thou anointest my head with oil; my cup runneth over.*
>
> *Surely goodness and mercy shall follow me all the days of my life and I shall dwell in the house of the Lord forever.*

An anointing with oil is symbolic of the anointing of the Holy Ghost. David was anointed with oil by Samuel as a teenager. From that time, the Spirit of the Lord came upon him, and the anointing grew in his life. It is because of the anointing that David was able to defeat Goliath and save Israel from a humiliating defeat at the hand of the Philistines. It was the anointing that caused David to prevail against Saul, even when Saul was after his life. He defeated all his enemies because of the anointing on his life. Because of the anointing on his life, he was Israel's best king.

1 John 2: 20, 27:

> *But ye have an unction from the Holy One, and ye know all things.*
>
> *But the anointing which ye have received of him abideth in you, and ye need not that any man teach you: but as the same anointing teacheth you of all things, and is truth and is no lie, and even as it hath taught you, ye shall abide in him.*

The Holy Spirit knows all things. He reveals to us what we need to know at the right time. Secret things belong to God, and He reveals them to whomsoever He will. The Holy Ghost is the unction for us to function according to the will of God. The Holy Spirit lives within us to help us whenever the need arises. We should always give Him the opportunity to assist us. The Holy Spirit is gentle. He will not override our will. The Holy Spirit will teach us and lead us into all truth, and through Him, we can have a dynamic, intimate relationship with Him.

www.ingramcontent.com/pod-product-compliance
Ingram Content Group UK Ltd.
Pitfield, Milton Keynes, MK11 3LW, UK
UKHW022216230426
12048UKWH00016BA/873